by
Barbara Getty & Inga Dubay

Handwriting Success™
Portland, Oregon USA

GETTY-DUBAY® ITALIC HANDWRITING SERIES

BOOK A ▪ Basic Italic
14 mm body height

BOOK B ▪ Basic Italic
11 mm, 9 mm body height

BOOK C ▪ Basic & Cursive Italic
9 mm, 6 mm body height   Introduction to Cursive Italic

BOOK D ▪ Basic & Cursive Italic
6 mm, 5 mm body height

BOOK E ▪ Basic & Cursive Italic
6 mm, 5 mm, 4 mm body height

BOOK F ▪ Basic & Cursive Italic
6 mm, 5 mm, 4 mm body height

BOOK G ▪ Basic & Cursive Italic
5 mm, 4 mm body height

INSTRUCTION MANUAL

INTERNATIONAL EDITION
Copyright 2012 by Barbara M. Getty and Inga S. Dubay
ISBN 978-0-9649215-9-7

FOURTH EDITION
Copyright 2012 by Barbara M. Getty and Inga S. Dubay
THIRD EDITION
Copyright 1994 by Barbara M. Getty and Inga S. Dubay
SECOND EDITION
Copyright 1986 by Barbara M. Getty and Inga S. Dubay
REVISED EDITION
Copyright 1980 by Barbara M. Getty and Inga S. Dubay
FIRST EDITION
Copyright 1979 by Barbara M. Getty and Inga S. Dubay

All rights reserved.
This text may not be reproduced in whole or in part
without the express written permission of the copyright holder.

Getty-Dubay is a registered trademark in the United States.

Published by Handwriting Success, LLC
Portland, Oregon USA

www.handwritingsuccess.com

Printed at various locations around the world by IngramSpark.

Cover Design: Sinda Markham
Front cover picture: Sitka spruce sprout from a "nurse log", white oxalis and swordfern
Back cover pictures: Checkerspot butterfly; Salal blossom

CONTENTS

iv	Introduction	26	Join 3 *ao*
v	Basic & Cursive Italic Alphabet	27	Review
vi	Reminders	28	Join 4 *ae*
viii	Assessment Pre-test/Post-test	29	Review
		30	Join 5 *on*
1	**PART 1: Getty-Dubay® Basic Italic**	35	Review
2	Families 1 & 2 *i j l · k v w x z*	36	Join 6 *rn*
3	Families 3 & 4 *n h m r · u y*	37	Review
4	Families 5 & 6 *a d g q · b p*	38	Join 7 *sn*
5	Families 7 & 8 *o e c s · f t*	39	Review
6	Capitals	40	Join 8 *aa*
7	Review, Numerals	42	Review
8	Uses of Basic Italic	43	Lifts
		44	Size, Slope, Spacing
9	**PART 2: Getty-Dubay® Cursive Italic**	45	Slope Guidelines, Timed Writing
10	Transition		
12	Overview of Joins	46	Cursive Capitals
16	Review, Cursive Capitals	53	Letter/Booklet
17	Join 1 *an*	54	Reading Looped Cursive
19	Review	55	5mm lines
20	Join 2 *au*	56	4mm lines
25	Review		

INTRODUCTION TO GETTY-DUBAY® ITALIC HANDWRITING

This is the fifth of seven workbooks in the *Getty-Dubay® Italic Handwriting Series*. It is recommended for fourth grade. This book is designed to provide further practice with cursive capitals and lowercase joins. For the student new to italic handwriting, an introduction to basic italic lowercase and capitals is provided, as well as an overview of the cursive joins. (The student may prefer to continue using basic capitals with lowercase cursive.)

Writing practice includes vowel sounds, consonant sounds, phonograms, prefixes, suffixes, and other letter combinations. Sentence content includes the six kingdoms of life, DNA, animal groups, minerals, photosynthesis, continents, biomes, our solar system, and galaxies. Cursive capital practice includes origins of our alphabet and cities of the world. Application form, letter/booklet format, and envelope making are also presented.

TEACHER/STUDENT INSTRUCTIONS: Writing process/stroke information, directions, notes, reminders, options, and assessments are included in the margins. Further letter and join descriptions and assessment questions are found in the INSTRUCTION MANUAL.

ASSESSMENT: Assessment is the key to improvement. The self-assessment method used enables the student to monitor progress. STEP 1: the student is asked to LOOK at the writing and affirm what is the best. Questions are asked requiring a yes/no answer. 'Yes' is affirmation of a task accomplished. 'No' indicates work to be done. STEP 2: the student is asked to PLAN what needs to be improved and how to accomplish this. STEP 3: the student is asked to put the plan into PRACTICE. This *LOOK, PLAN, PRACTICE* format provides self-assessment skills applicable to all learning situations. Letter shape is the first focus. The next focus is on size, spacing, and slope.

Eventually the student has a checklist: letter shape, letter size, letter spacing, and letter slope. Use the *Slope Guidelines* to enable the student to find a personal slope choice. Speed is encouraged after letterforms and joins are learned. *Timed Writing* enables a gradual increase in the number of words written per minute while maintaining comfort and legibility. Repeat *Timed Writing* once a month. *Reading Looped Cursive* provides experience reading another writing style, while comparing legibility with italic handwriting.

CLASSROOM MANAGEMENT: Using direct instruction, present two pages a week, with follow-up practice on lined paper. Demonstrate the process/stroke sequence for letters and joins. This instruction, together with opportunities for integrating handwriting into other areas of curriculum, can provide 20 to 30 minutes, 3 to 4 times a week. From day one, have DESK STRIPS and WALL CHART in place. For extra practice use BLACKLINE MASTERS. Have lined paper available that matches the 5mm and 4mm lines used in this book (see *Reminders*). Lines at the back of this book and in the INSTRUCTION MANUAL may be duplicated. The student may write on the lines provided in this book or use thin paper for tracing over models in the book. Provide the opportunity for each student to select a page of his/her best handwriting to include in the student's portfolio.

This Fourth Edition includes join options and lift options for students to consider.

As a teacher, your interest and enthusiasm are instrumental in attaining the goal of legible and neat handwriting. The enjoyment of good handwriting is shared by both the writer and the reader. Handwriting is a lifelong skill. Good handwriting is a lifelong joy!

N.B. The information sources for the writing practice are: *The New Reading Teacher's Book of Lists*;, Rand McNally World Atlas; *Physical Science*, Prentice-Hall, 2006; *Biology*, Holt, 2008; *Biology: Understanding Life*, Alters & Alters. 2006. Source for origins of the alphabet is *Ancient Writing & Its Influence*, Berthold Ullman.

GETTY-DUBAY® ITALIC HANDWRITING SERIES
BASIC & CURSIVE ITALIC ALPHABET

BASIC ITALIC

*All letters written in one stroke unless otherwise indicated. All letters start at the top except lowercase **d** and **e**.*

Aa Bb Cc Dd Ee Ff Gg

Hh Ii Jj Kk Ll Mm

Nn Oo Pp Qq Rr Ss Tt

Uu Vv Ww Xx Yy Zz

0 1 2 3 4 5 6 7 8 9

CURSIVE ITALIC

*All letters written in one stroke unless otherwise indicated. All letters start at the top except lowercase **d** and **e**.*

Aa Bb Cc Dd Ee Ff Gg

ana bnb cnc dnd ene fnf gng
or ene

Hh Ii Jj Kk Ll Mm

hnh ini jnj knk lnl mnm
or knk   or mnm

Nn Oo Pp Qq Rr Ss Tt

nnn ono pnp qnq rnr sns tnt
or nnn   or rnr or sns

Uu Vv Ww Xx Yy Zz

unu vnv wnw xnx yny znz
or xnx

GETTY-DUBAY® ITALIC HANDWRITING REMINDERS

PENCIL HOLD
Use a soft lead pencil (#1 or #2) with an eraser. Hold the pencil with the thumb and index finger, resting on the middle finger. The upper part of the pencil rests near the large knuckle.

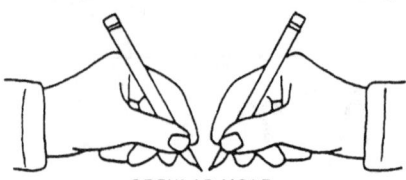
REGULAR HOLD

Hold the pencil firmly and lightly. AVOID pinching. To relax your hand, tap the index finger on the pencil three times.

Problem grips such as the 'thumb wrap' (thumb doesn't touch pencil) and the 'death grip' (very tight pencil hold) make it difficult to use the hand's small muscles. To relieve these problems, try this alternative pencil hold.

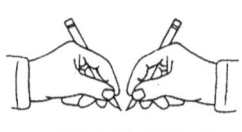
ALTERNATIVE HOLD

Place the pencil between the index finger and the middle finger. The pencil rests between the index and middle fingers by the large knuckles. Hold the pencil in the regular way at the tips of the fingers.

PAPER POSITION

LEFT-HANDED
If you are left-handed and write with the wrist below the line of writing, turn the paper clockwise so it is slanted to the right as illustrated. If you are left-handed and write with a "hook" with the wrist above the line of writing, turn the paper counter clockwise so it is slanted to the left as illustrated. (Similar to the right-handed position)

RIGHT-HANDED
If you are right-handed turn the paper counter-clockwise so it is slanted to the left as illustrated.

POSTURE
Rest your feet flat on the floor and keep your back comfortably straight without slumping. Rest your forearms on the desk. Hold the workbook or paper with your non-writing hand so that the writing area is centered in front of you.

LINED PAPER CHOICES:
The following choices for lined paper may be used when instructions say use lined paper for practice.

1. Lines 5mm body height on page 55 may be duplicated. These lines can also be used as guidelines under a sheet of unlined paper. Fasten with paper clips.

   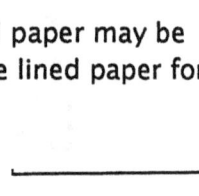

2. Lines 4 mm body height on page 56 may be duplicated. These lines can also be used as a line guide under a sheet of unlined paper.

   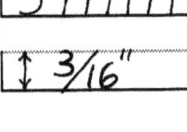

3. Some school paper has a solid baseline and a dotted waistline. Use paper with a body height of 6mm ($^1/_4$") or 5mm ($^3/_{16}$").

   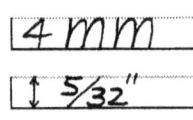

4. Some school paper has only baselines. Use paper with lines 12mm ($^1/_2$") or 10mm ($^3/_8$") apart.

   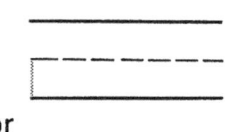

5. Use wide-ruled notebook paper with a space of about 9 mm ($^3/_8$") between lines. Create your own waistline by lining up two sheets of notebook paper and shifting one down half a space. The faint line showing through will serve as a waistline. Fasten with paper clips.

   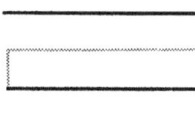
   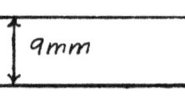
   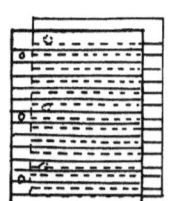

Getty-Dubay® Italic Handwriting Reminders

VOCABULARY

[Vocabulary chart showing labeled letterform terms: waistline, baseline, body height, ascender height, capital height, downstroke, arch, basic a shape, elliptical curve, crossbar, branching line, descender length, counter, diagonal, inverted arch, inverted basic a shape, curve entrance serif, dot or jot, exit serif, entrance serif, soft angle, sharp angle, diagonal joins, horizontal join, curve exit serif — illustrated with letters: i j A a l v n u a b o f / a i r w a n a e m o n R]

STROKES

Basic italic letters all start at the top and go down or over (horizontal), except **d** and **e**, (**d** starts at the waistline and **e** starts at the center of the body height). Follow the direction of the arrow. Letters are written in one stroke unless otherwise indicated. Trace the dotted line model, then copy model in space provided. If needed, trace solid line model.

LETTER DIMENSIONS

SHAPE
Basic italic lowercase letters are divided into eight families according to shape. Basic italic capitals are divided into three width groups. Cursive italic lowercase joins are divided into eight join groups.

SIZE
Letters are written with a consistent body height. Capitals, ascenders and descenders are written one and a half times the body height.

SLOPE
The models are written with a 5° letter slope. A consistent slope is an important part of good handwriting. For individual slope choices see *Slope Guidelines*, page 45.

SPACING
Letters are written close together within words. Joins are natural spacers in cursive italic; when lifts occur, keep letters close together. Spacing between words is the width of an **n** in basic and cursive italic.

SPEED
Write at a comfortable rate of speed. Though speed is not a primary concern at this level, students may use the *Timed Writing*, page 45.

GOAL
To write legible, neat handwriting.

IMPROVEMENT
Assessment is the key to improving your handwriting. Follow this improvement method as you learn basic and cursive italic handwriting.

1. **LOOK** at your writing. Circle your best letter or join. Answer question about strokes, shape, size, spacing, or slope.

2. **PLAN** how to make your writing look more like the model. Pick the letter or join that needs work. Compare with the model.

3. **PRACTICE** the letter or join that needs work. Write on the lines provided and on lined paper.

 Give yourself a star at the top of the page when you see you have made an improvement.

NOTE: See INSTRUCTION MANUAL, Assessment, pp. 54-68.

Getty-Dubay® Pre-test/Post-test

INFORMAL ASSESSMENT OF STUDENT PROGRESS

The main purpose of handwriting instruction is to promote legibility so that we can communicate with others and ourselves.

PRE-TEST Before you begin this book, write the following sentence in your everyday handwriting. Also write your name, address and today's date.

A quick brown fox jumps over the lazy dog.

POST-TEST After you have completed this workbook, write the following sentence in cursive italic. Also write your name, address and today's date in cursive italic.

A quick brown fox jumps over the lazy dog.

ASSESSMENT
- SHAPE: Each letter is similar to the models in the workbook.
- SIZE: Similar letters are the same height (for example: aec, dhk, gpy). Capital letters and lowercase letters with ascenders are the same height.
- SLOPE: Letters have a consistent letter slope (between 5° – 15°).
- SPACING: Letters within words are closely spaced. Spaces between words are the width of **n**.
- SPEED: Words are written fluently at a comfortable speed.

PART I

GETTY-DUBAY® BASIC ITALIC

LOWERCASE: 8 families

Family 1. straight line downstroke - i j l
Family 2. diagonal line - k v w x z
Family 3. arch - n h m r
Family 4. inverted arch - u y
Family 5. basic *a* shape - a d g q
Family 6. inverted basic *a* shape - b p
Family 7. elliptical curve - o e c s
Family 8. crossbar - f t

Improvement: shape, size

CAPITALS: 3 width groups

1. wide width - C G O Q D M W
2. medium width - T H A N K U V X Y Z
3. narrow width - E F L B P R S J I

Improvement: shape, size

LOWERCASE AND CAPITALS

Improvement: size, slope, spacing

NUMERALS

abcdefghijklmnopqrstuvwxyz

GETTY-DUBAY® BASIC ITALIC LOWERCASE

NOTE: Can you tell how letters in each family are alike?

NOTE: All letters start at the top and go down or over, except **d** and **e**.

Family 1: i j l
Family 2: k v w x z
Family 3: n h m r
Family 4: u y
Family 5: a d g q
Family 6: b p
Family 7: o e c s
Family 8: f t

FAMILY 1: STRAIGHT LINE DOWNSTROKE

Trace and copy.

i j l

descender length and ascender height

✏ Circle your best **i, j,** and **l**.

FAMILY 2: DIAGONAL LINE

k v w x z

k k k k   k
v v v   v
w w w   w
x x x   x
z z z   z
kiwi kiwi   kiwi

HINT: The corner of a sheet of paper fits here. This is a right angle.

baseline

✏ Circle your best **k, v, w, x,** and **z**.

NOTE: For assessment questions see INSTRUCTION MANUAL.

Getty-Dubay® Italic Handwriting Series · Book E   © 2012 Getty-Dubay

Getty-Dubay® Basic Italic Lowercase

FAMILY 3: ARCH

Trace and copy.

nhmr

imaginary branching line

NOTE: arch
branch out at imaginary branching line

n n n   n
h h h   h
m m m   m
r r r   r
rim rim   rim

✏️ Circle your best **h, m, n,** and **r**.

FAMILY 4: INVERTED ARCH (UPSIDE-DOWN ARCH)

u y

branching line

NOTE:
upside down arch
branch in at imaginary branching line

u u u   u
y y y   y
hum hum   hum
run run   run
lily lily   lily

[1] LOOK at your writing. Pick your best letters.

✏️ Circle your best **u** and **y**.

[2] Pick the letters that need work. Compare them with the models. PLAN how to make them look more like the models.

[3] PRACTICE

HINT:

n Turn n upside down to see u.

© 2012 Getty-Dubay

Getty-Dubay® Basic Italic Lowercase

FAMILY 5: BASIC *a* SHAPE

a d g q

Trace and copy.

a a a   a

branch in at imaginary branching line

d d d   d

NOTE: branch in at imaginary branching line

a shape

g g g   g

HINT: flat head

q q q   q

and and   and

soft angle (chin) curve

aqua aqua   aqua

NOTE:
Close up the top of **a**, **d**, **g**, and **q** so that
a doesn't look like **u**,
d doesn't look like **cl**,
and **g** & **q** don't look like **y**.

a u   d d   g y   q q   ✏ Circle your best **a**, **d**, **g**, and **q**.

FAMILY 6: INVERTED BASIC *a* SHAPE (UPSIDE-DOWN BASIC *a* SHAPE)

b p

b b b   b

imaginary branching line

p p p   p

NOTE:
branch out at imaginary branching line

bump bump   bump

upside-down a shape

✏ Circle your best **b** and **p**.

HINTS:

Turn **d** upside down to see **p**.

d

Turn **q** upside down to see **b**.

q

Getty-Dubay® Italic Handwriting Series · Book E

Getty-Dubay® Basic Italic Lowercase

FAMILY 7: ELLIPTICAL CURVE

o e c s   Trace and copy.

o o o   o

imaginary branching line

e e e   e

NOTE:
e center of body height

c c c   c

s s s   s

NOTE:
Close up the top of **o** so that **o** doesn't look like **u**.

oceans oceans   oceans

✏️ Circle your best **o, e, c,** and **s**.

FAMILY 8: CROSSBAR

f t

f f f   f

t t t   t

fast fast   fast

ft ft ft ft   ft

lift lift   lift

NOTE:
The crossbar joins **f** and **t**.

ft Ascender of **t** is shorter than the ascender of **f**.

✏️ Circle your best **f** and **t**.

1️⃣ LOOK at your writing.

2️⃣ PLAN which letters need work. How will you make them look more like the models?

3️⃣ PRACTICE the letters that need more work.

© 2012 Getty-Dubay   5   Getty-Dubay® Italic Handwriting Series · Book E

GETTY-DUBAY® BASIC ITALIC CAPITALS:
WIDE, MEDIUM and NARROW

Trace and copy.

WIDE

C G O Q D M W

width equals height

M and W slightly wider

C G O Q D M W

capital height

✏️ Are your **C, G, O, Q,** and **D** wide?   Yes___ No___

✏️ Are your **M** and **W** slightly wider?   Yes___ No___

PRACTICE letters here and on lined paper.

NOTE: All capitals start at the top.

MEDIUM

T H A N K U V X Y Z

width is ⁴/₅ of height

T H A N K U V X Y Z

HINT: To help remember the medium width letters they spell "Thank U (you) V, X, Y, and Z".

✏️ Are your letters medium width?   Yes___ No___

PRACTICE letters here and on lined paper.

NOTE: For Basic Italic Capital assessment, see INSTRUCTION MANUAL.

Getty-Dubay® Italic Handwriting Series · Book E   © 2012 Getty-Dubay

Getty-Dubay® Basic Italic Capitals, Lowercase, and Numerals

NARROW

width is ½ of height

Trace and copy.

E F L B P R S J I

E F L B P R S J I

NOTE: All capitals start at the top.

✏ Are your letters narrow width?   Yes___ No___

PRACTICE letters here and on lined paper.

REVIEW: BASIC ITALIC CAPITALS AND LOWERCASE

Aa Bb Cc Dd Ee Ff Gg

A

Hh Ii Jj Kk Ll Mm Nn

Oo Pp Qq Rr Ss Tt Uu

Vv Ww Xx Yy Zz

① LOOK at your writing. Pick your best letters.

② Pick the letters that need work. Compare them with the models. PLAN how to make them look more like the models.

③ Place lined paper over the models and trace. PRACTICE on lined paper.

NUMERALS: The size of numerals is one body height.

0 1 2 3 4 4 5 5 6 7 8 9 10 11 12

O

NOTE: For origins of numerals see Getty-Dubay® Italic Handwriting Series Instruction Manual, page 44.

PANGRAM: A sentence containing all the letters in the alphabet. Trace and copy.

Body height is 5mm (previous body height was 6mm).

A quick brown fox jumps over the lazy dog. A

SLOPE: Straight line downstrokes are parallel to 5° slope.

A qui

See Slope Guidelines on page 45.

PRACTICE writing with an even slope.

SPACING: There are three widths of spacing letters in words:

1. Wide space between straight line downstrokes.
2. Medium space between straight line and curve.
3. Narrow space between two curves at the center. Narrow space between diagonal and downstroke at the waistline.

hill
home
pod
wavy

PRACTICE writing using even letter spacing.

PRACTICE writing using the width of an n between words.

Leave the width of n between words.

USING BASIC ITALIC

Basic italic, sometimes called "printing", is useful for many writing purposes, such as messages, posters, maps, announcements, recipes, and for filling out application forms. When a form says "Please print", use basic italic.

Complete this application form using your best basic italic handwriting.

APPLICATION FORM Please print

Name: _____
               Last   First   Middle

Address: _____
               Street

_____
               City   State   Zip Code

School: _____ Age: _____

PART 2

GETTY-DUBAY® CURSIVE ITALIC

TRANSITION TO CURSIVE ITALIC

*Addition: descender for **f***
*Options: dot or jot for **i** and **j**, two-stroke **k** or one-stroke **k***
*Serifs: soft angle exit serifs - **a d h i k l u n m z***
*soft angle entrance serifs - **r n m x z***
*sharp angle entrance serifs - **j p v w***

Improvement: shape

CURSIVE ITALIC LOWERCASE: 8 JOINS

Join 1. diagonal - an
Join 2. diagonal swing up - au
Join 3. diagonal start back - ao
Join 4. diagonal into e - ae
Join 5. horizontal - on
Join 6. diagonal out of r - ru
Join 7. horizontal to diagonal - sn
Join 8. diagonal to horizontal - aa
Lifts - lift before f and z; lift after g j q y
Review

Vowel sounds, consonant sounds, phonograms, prefixes, suffixes, letter and envelope writing

Improvement: shape, size, spacing, slope

CURSIVE CAPITALS

Origins: Egyptian, Phoenician, Greek, Roman
Basic Italic and Cursive Italic
Writing practice using cities of the world

Improvement: shape, size, slope

READING LOOPED CURSIVE

Comparison of cursive italic handwriting with looped cursive handwriting

SLOPE, SPEED

Slope Guidelines
Timed Writing

LINES

5mm, 4mm

abcdefghijklmnopqrstuvwxyz

GETTY-DUBAY® ITALIC HANDWRITING SERIES
TRANSITION FROM BASIC ITALIC TO CURSIVE ITALIC

ADDITION & OPTIONS:

ADDITION: f adds a descender
f·f

OPTION: i and j use a dot or jot
i·i or i   j·j or j

OPTION: k may also be a one-stroke letter
k·k or k

SERIFS: Serifs are lines added to letters.
There are exit serifs and entrance serifs.

Serifs are like hands reaching out to join letters.

EXIT SERIF: End with a soft angle at the baseline into a short diagonal. (n, m, and x also have entrance serifs.)

← diagonal
↑ soft angle

a·a a   d·d d
h·h h   i·i i
k·k k   l·l l
m·m m   n·n n
u·u u   x·x x

AVOID a hook
AVOID a scoop

1 LOOK at your writing. Pick your best letters. Answer the question.

✏ Circle some of your best exit serifs.   Yes___ No___

✏ Are your letters ending with a soft angle exit serif?   Yes___ No___

2 Pick the letters that need work. Compare them with the models. PLAN how to make them look more like the models.

3 PRACTICE here the letters that need work.

Getty-Dubay® Italic Handwriting Series · Book E   © 2012 Getty-Dubay

Transition from Basic Italic to Cursive Italic

ENTRANCE SERIFS:

There are two kinds of entrance serifs—soft angle entrance serifs and sharp angle entrance serifs.

SOFT ANGLE
ENTRANCE SERIF: Begin with a short diagonal line to a soft angle. (m, n, and x have exit serifs also)

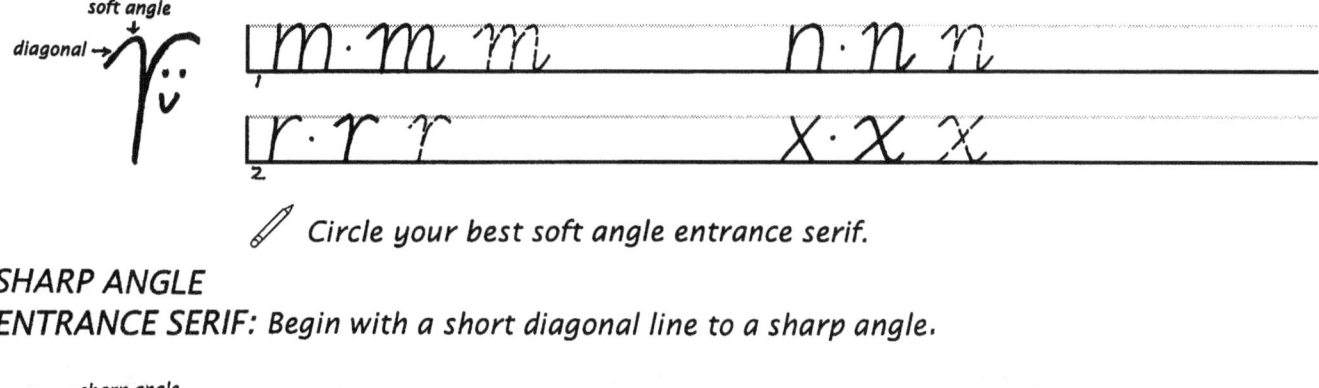

✏ Circle your best soft angle entrance serif.

SHARP ANGLE
ENTRANCE SERIF: Begin with a short diagonal line to a sharp angle.

✏ Circle your best sharp angle entrance serif.

PRACTICE the letters that need more work.

AVOID a scoop

CURSIVE Z: Add short entrance and exit serifs to z.

✏ Circle your best z.

REVIEW: CURSIVE ITALIC LOWERCASE LETTERS

No change: b, c, e, g, o, q, s, t, and y.

[1] Trace and copy. LOOK at your writing.

[2] PLAN which letters need work.

[3] PRACTICE those letters on lined paper.

© 2012 Getty-Dubay   11   Getty-Dubay® Italic Handwriting Series · Book E

GETTY-DUBAY® CURSIVE ITALIC LOWERCASE JOINS OVERVIEW

JOIN 1: DIAGONAL Join with a straight diagonal line.

an Trace and copy.

an an an an   an

Serifs are like hands reaching out to join letters.

in in in in   in

en en en   en

un un un un   un

em   er   ex

em

im   ir   ix

im

um um   ur   ux

✏ Are you using a straight diagonal line for the join?   Yes___ No___

1. LOOK at your writing. Answer the question.
2. PLAN which joins need work. How will you make them look more like the models?
3. PRACTICE the joins that need more work.

JOIN 2: DIAGONAL SWING UP Join with a straight diagonal line.

au

au au au au   au

Serifs reach out to join letters.

ay   ai   at

ay   ai   at

Getty-Dubay® Italic Handwriting Series · Book E

Getty-Dubay® Cursive Italic Lowercase Joins Overview

Trace and copy.   aj aj   ap ap
                   av av   aw aw

Serifs reach out to join letters with ascenders.

                   al al al al

imaginary branching line   ah ah   ak ak   ab ab
                           el el   eh eh   eb eb   ek ek

✎ Are you joining at the imaginary branching line? Yes___ No___

OPTION: Join into n, m, r, and x with Diagonal Swing Up.

                   an an   am am
                   ar ar   ax ax
                   en en   em em   er er   ex ex

JOIN 3: DIAGONAL START BACK Join with a straight diagonal line.

ao   ao ao ao ao   Serifs reach up to the waistline.
          eo eo   io io   uo uo

✎ Are you joining into o with a straight diagonal line? Yes___ No___

OPTION: Join into s from the baseline to the waistline,
leaving off the horizontal top of s.

                   as as   es es
                   is is   us us

OPTION: See Join 8 where the s shape is unchanged.

                   as as   es es   is is   us us

PRACTICE the joins
that need more work.

© 2012 Getty-Dubay   13   Getty-Dubay® Italic Handwriting Series · Book E

Getty-Dubay® Cursive Italic Lowercase Joins Overview

JOIN 4: DIAGONAL INTO e Join with a diagonal line.

ae ae ae ae ae   ae

Trace and copy.   Join out of e into all letters (except f and z).

ee ee   ie ie   ue ue

✏️ Are you joining into e at the branching line?   Yes___ No___

OPTION: Lift before e from baseline.

ae ae   ee ee   ie ie   ue ue

JOIN 5: HORIZONTAL Join with a horizontal line at the waistline.

ou ou ou ou ou   ou

Reach out along the waistline.

on on   oo oo   oa oa

tu tu tu   tu   Reach out from the crossbar.

fo fo   fa fa

vi wi vi wi   xi xi

✏️ Are you joining with a horizontal join out of o, t, f, v, and x? Yes___ No___

OPTION: Join into e from crossbar at the waistline.   te te fe fe

OPTION: Join into e out of the first stroke of t.   te te

OPTION: Lift before e from waistline.   te te   fe fe

NOTE: When lifting between letters be sure to keep letters close together.
Joins are natural spacers -- when not using a join keep letters close.

Getty-Dubay® Italic Handwriting Series · Book E   © 2012 Getty-Dubay

Getty-Dubay® Cursive Italic Lowercase Joins Overview

JOIN 6: DIAGONAL OUT OF r Join with a short diagonal line.

ru   ru ru ru ru   ru

Trace and copy.   It's just a short reach out of r.

rn rn   ro ro   ra ra   re re

✏ Are you joining out of r with a short diagonal line?   Yes___ No___

OPTION: Lift after r.

ru ru   rn rn   ro ro   ra ra

JOIN 7: HORIZONTAL TO DIAGONAL Join with a horizontal line blending into a diagonal line.

sn   sn sn sn sn   sn

su su   so so   bo po

se   be   pe   Follow back out of s, b, and p.

se   be   pe

OPTION: Lift after s, b, and p.

sn sn   bo bo   po po   be be

JOIN 8: DIAGONAL TO HORIZONTAL Join with a diagonal line blending into a horizontal line.

aa   aa aa aa aa   aa

ac ad ag aq as   Reach out to join into a, c, d, g, q, and s.

ac

OPTION: Lift before a, c, d, g, q, and s when joining from the baseline.

aa aa ac ac ad ad ag ag aq aq as as

LIFTS: Lift before f and lift before z from baseline. Lift after g, j, q, and y.

Getty-Dubay® Cursive Italic Lowercase Joins Overview

REVIEW: GETTY-DUBAY® CURSIVE ITALIC LOWERCASE JOINS

JOIN 1 an an an (OPTION)   JOIN 2 au au (OPTION)
JOIN 3 ao ao as (OPTION)   JOIN 4 ae ae ae (OPTION)
JOIN 5 on on   JOIN 6 ru ru ru (OPTION)
JOIN 7 sn sn sn (OPTION)   JOIN 8 aa aa aa (OPTION)

Body height is 5mm (previous body height was 6mm).

REVIEW: GETTY-DUBAY® CURSIVE ITALIC CAPITALS AND LOWERCASE

The letter n is used to show how to join into and out of letters.

Aana Bbnb Ccnc Ddnd
      or na   or bn   or nc   or nd
A   B   C   D

NOTE: Basic italic capitals may be used with cursive italic lowercase if preferred to cursive capitals.

Eene Ffnf Ggng Hhnh
or ne   or ng
E   F   G   H

NOTE: For further practice of capitals see pages 46 – 52.

Iini Jjnj Kknk or knk Llnl
I   J   K   L

Mmnm Nnnn Oono Ppnp
or mnm   or nnn   or pn
M   N   O   P

1. LOOK at your writing. Pick your best letters.

Qqnq Rrnr Ssns or sns Ttnt
or nq   or rnr
Q   R   S   T

2. Pick the letters that need work. Compare them with the models. PLAN how to make them look more like the models.

Uunu Vvnv Wwnw Xxnx
                              or nx
U   V   W   X

3. PRACTICE the letters that need more work.

Yyny Zznz   Y   Z

A quick brown fox jumps over the lazy dog. A q

For Cursive Italic Capitals and Lowercase assessment see INSTRUCTION MANUAL pp. 65–66.

GETTY-DUBAY® CURSIVE ITALIC LOWERCASE JOINS
JOIN 1: DIAGONAL

Join 1 is a straight diagonal line from the baseline to the waistline into **n**, **m**, **r**, and **x**.

a *an*
diagonal to soft angle

an | an en in kn mn un
Trace & copy. an

Double n / Silent n
nn running n autumn
nn

PREFIX: en- / SUFFIX: -en
en- encourage -en taken
en

CONSONANT SOUND: KN: N sound / PREFIX: un-
kn know un- unusual
kn

PREFIX: in-
in- include · insect
in

lacewing

✎ Circle your best diagonal join into **n**.

a *am*
diagonal to soft angle

am | am em im mm um
am

PREFIX: im- / Double m
im- impatient mm mammal
im

✎ Circle your best diagonal join into **m**.

PRACTICE here and on lined paper.

NOTE: AVOID a wavy line
im

✎ Are you using a straight line for your diagonal join?   Yes___ No___

✎ Are you AVOIDING a wavy line?   Yes___ No___

© 2012 Getty-Dubay   17   Getty-Dubay® Italic Handwriting Series · Book E

Getty-Dubay® Cursive Italic Lowercase Joins

a͡r a͡r
diagonal
to soft angle

ar Trace & copy. ar cr dr er ir kr ur
ar

VOWEL SOUNDS:
AR: AIR sound
AR: AR sound

ar care ar larva
ar

ER: R sound
IR: R sound

er mineral ir girl
er

UR: R sound
PHONOGRAM: * -ur

ur murmur -ur fur
ur

CONSONANT SOUNDS:
CR: CR blend
DR: DR blend
SUFFIX: -er

cr crab dr draw -er smaller
cr

Metamorphosis:
egg to larva (caterpillar)
to chrysalis (pupa)
to adult butterfly

— egg
— larva
— chrysalis
— butterfly

✏ Circle your best diagonal join into **r**.

a͡x a͡x
diagonal
to soft angle

ax Trace and copy. ax ex ix ux x x
ax

PREFIX: ex-
PHONOGRAM: -ax

ex exist explore -ax thorax
ex

CONSONANT SOUND:
X: KS sound

x mix next lynx
x

head
thorax
abdomen

wingless wasp

All insects have six legs (thorax area). Some insects have wings; others are wingless.

✏ Circle your best diagonal join into **x**.

* PHONOGRAM: A phonogram is a vowel sound plus a consonant sound. It is often less than a syllable. It needs an initial consonant or blend to make it a word.

All insects have a three-part body:
head, thorax, and abdomen.

Getty-Dubay® Italic Handwriting Series · Book E

Getty-Dubay® Cursive Italic Lowercase Joins

REVIEW: JOIN 1

JOIN 1 joins are underlined.

NOTE:
Write **t** and **e** close together. AVOID a gap between **t** & **e**.

The six kingdoms of life are:
Animalia, Archaebacteria, Eubacteria,
Fungi, Plantae, and Protista.

✏ Circle one of your best diagonal joins.

OPTION: Join into **n**, **m**, **r**, and **x** with Diagonal Swing Up

an am ar ax · en em er ex · in im ir ix

un um ur ux · nn mm rr · and · are

NOTE:
Optional join (Join 2) into **n**, **m**, **r**, & **x** used here.

All insects have a three-part body:
head, thorax, and abdomen.

The six kingdoms of life are:
Animalia, Archaebacteria, Eubacteria,
Fungi, Plantae, and Protista.

1️⃣ LOOK at your writing. Pick your best join. Answer the question.

2️⃣ Pick the joins that need work. Compare them with the models. PLAN how to make the joins look more like the models.

3️⃣ PRACTICE those joins here and on lined paper.

Getty-Dubay® Cursive Italic Lowercase Joins

JOIN 2: DIAGONAL SWING UP

*Join 2 is a straight diagonal line from the baseline to the branching line, then swing up to the waistline or ascender height into **b, h, i, j, k, l, p, t, u, v, w,** and **y**. Optional join into **n, m, r,** and **x**.*

a ↗ au
diagonal swing up

au | au cu du eu hu iu ku lu
Trace & copy. au

Letters join at the branching line.
imaginary branching line

mu nu zu · **Double u** uu vacuum
mu

VOWEL SOUND:
AU: broad O

au caution dinosaur
au

Tyrannosaurus Rex

✏ Circle one of your best joins into **u**.

a ↗ ay
diagonal swing up

ay | ay cy dy ey iy ky ly my
ay

SUFFIX: -ly

ny uy -ly slowly neatly
ny

VOWEL SOUND:
AY: long A
SUFFIX: -cy

ay clay layer -cy accuracy
ay

SUFFIX: -y

-y cloudy rainy sunny
y

✏ Circle one of your best joins into **y**.

PRACTICE the joins that need more work.

Getty-Dubay® Italic Handwriting Series · Book E

Getty-Dubay® Cursive Italic Lowercase Joins

a↗ ai
diagonal
swing up

| ai | ai ci di ei hi ki li mi ni |

Trace & copy. ai

Double i
PHONOGRAM: -ain

ii zi · ii skiing -ain brain

ii

VOWEL SOUND:
AI: long A
PHONOGRAM: -air

ai aid rain -air hair pair

ai

✎ Circle your best join into **i**.

a↗ aj
a↗ ap
diagonal
swing up

PHONOGRAMS:
-ap, -amp, -ump.

| aj ap | aj ap ej ep ip lp mp up |

aj

-ap map -amp lamp -ump lump

ap

✎ Circle your best join into **p** and **j**.

NOTE:
Optional join (Join 2) into **n**, **m**, **r**, & **x** used here.

DNA - deoxyribonucleic acid

D

DNA is in all living things.

D

DNA contains the blueprint for life
written in a genetic code: A (Adenine),
C (Cytosine), G (Guanine), and
T (Thymine).

© 2012 Getty-Dubay

Getty-Dubay® Cursive Italic Lowercase Joins

a→at
diagonal swing up

at | Trace & copy. at ct et it lt nt ut
at

PHONOGRAMS: -at, -int
-at cat mat that -int print

REMINDER: t has a short ascender.
at

SUFFIX: -ant
Double t
-ant assistant tt spotted

NOTE: DOUBLE T
long crossbar
ant

U tt
large U shape

✏ Does your **t** have a short ascender?   Yes___   No___

a→al
diagonal swing up

al | al cl el il ll ul · Silent l half
al

VOWEL SOUND: AL: broad O
PHONOGRAM: -all
al always salt -all small
al

PHONOGRAMS: -ell, -ill, -ull
-ell shell -ill hill -ull gull
ell

CONSONANT SOUND: CL: CL blend
PHONOGRAM: -ilt
cl clear include -ilt quilt
cl

SUFFIXES: -al, -ily
-al natural -ily happily

NOTE:
imaginary branching line
Join into l at the branching line.
at

al

✏ Circle one of your best joins into **l**.

AVOID
al
scoop and loop

Getty-Dubay® Italic Handwriting Series · Book E   22   © 2012 Getty-Dubay

Getty-Dubay® Cursive Italic Lowercase Joins

a↗ ah
diagonal swing up

| ah | ah ch eh ih uh h honest |

Trace & copy.

CONSONANT SOUND:
CH: digraph

ch lunch chipmunk

✏ Circle your best join into **h**.

a↗ ab
diagonal swing up

Silent **b**

| ab | ab eb ib lb mb ub **b** thumb |

PHONOGRAMS: -ab, -ib, -ub, -umb

-ab crab -ib rib -ub cub -umb

Write your own word using the phonogram -umb.

✏ Circle your best join into **b**.

a↗ ak
diagonal swing up

| ak | ak ck ek ik lk nk uk or uk |

Silent k
PHONOGRAM: -ank

k knowledge -ank sank clank

PHONOGRAMS: -ink, -unk, -alk, -ick

-ink sink clink -unk sunk clunk

-alk talk -ick pick flicker

✏ Circle your best join into **k**.

PRACTICE here and on lined paper.

Getty-Dubay® Cursive Italic Lowercase Joins

a͡v a͡v
a͡v a͡v
diagonal swing up

VOWEL SOUND:
AW: broad O

PHONOGRAM: -ew

OPTION: v and w may be written with either a sharp angle or a soft angle at the baseline.

av aw | av aw ev ew iv iw
Trace & copy. | sharp angle v ... sharp angle w
| av

aw awe claw -ew few knew
aw

av aw ev ew iv iw claw
soft angle v   soft angle w
av

✎ Circle your best join into v and w.

Quagga (South Africa) extinct since the 19th century.

5° SLOPE

Many species have vanished from our Earth. Many cases of extinction are due to environmental change.

PRACTICE writing with an even slope.

See Slope Guidelines on page 45.

✎ Are you using a 5° slope? Yes___ No___

OPTION: Join into n, m, r, and x with Diagonal Swing Up

Join at the imaginary branching line.

imaginary branching line →

an am ar ax · en em er ex · in im
an

ir ix · un um ur ux · nn mm
ir

NOTE: Optional join (Join 2) into n, m, r, & x used here.

Many species have vanished from our Earth. Many cases of extinction are due to environmental change.

Getty-Dubay® Italic Handwriting Series · Book E

Getty-Dubay® Cursive Italic Lowercase Joins

REVIEW: JOIN 2

JOIN 2 joins are underlined.

NOTE:
Optional Join 2 into **n**, **m**, **r** and **x** also included.

In the Kingdom Animalia, more than one million known species of animals exist.

Some phyla or subgroups within this kingdom are: Mammals, Birds, Reptiles, Amphibians, Fishes (Bony and Cartilaginous), and Arthropods.

Other phyla in Kingdom Animalia are: Lancelets, Echinoderms, Mollusks, Segmented Worms, Flatworms, Roundworms, Cnidarians, & Sponges.

* Crustaceans have one set of appendages per segment.

Arthropods are the largest animal group on Earth. This group includes insects (six legs), arachnids (eight legs), and crustaceans.*

1. LOOK at your writing.

2. Pick the joins that need work. Compare them with the models. PLAN how to make the joins look more like the models.

3. PRACTICE the joins that need more work.

Arthropods are great recyclers and decomposers. They also help pollinate the plants that provide food and keep the air and water clean.

NOTE: Have you made an improvement in your handwriting? Pick a page of your best handwriting to put in your Student Portfolio.

JOIN 3: DIAGONAL START BACK

Join 3 is a straight diagonal line from the baseline to the waistline then start back into **o**.

a/ ao
diagonal
start back

ao | ao co do eo ho io ko lo
Trace & copy. ao

PREFIX: co-

mo no uo zo   co- cooperate
mo

VOWEL SOUND:
O: short O

o copy oxygen
o

VOWEL SOUND:
O: long O

o open potato
o

AVOID wave
ao

Photosynthesis (sunlight, carbon dioxide, oxygen, water)

✏️ Circle one of your best diagonal joins into **o**.

OPTION: Join into **s** from the baseline to the waistline, leaving off the horizontal top of **s**.

a/ as
diagonal
start back

as cs ds es hs is ks or ks ls
as

Silent s

ms ns us zs   s islands
ms

CONSONANT
SOUNDS:
S: regular
S: Z sound

s us this   s is has does
s

PREFIX: dis-, mis-

dis- disability mis- misuse
dis

✏️ Circle one of your best diagonal joins into **s**.

PRACTICE here and
on lined paper.

Getty-Dubay® Cursive Italic Lowercase Joins

OPTION: Join into **s** from the baseline to the waistline, leaving the horizontal top of **s**.

NOTE:
See Join 8, page 42.

as cs ds es hs is ks or ks ls ms ns
as

us zs s islands isle aisle
us

CONSONANT
SOUNDS:
S: regular
S: Z sound

s us this s is has does
s

PREFIX: dis-, mis-

dis- disability mis- misuse
dis

✏️ Circle one of your best joins into **s** using a diagonal into the horizontal top of **s**.

REVIEW: JOIN 3

JOIN 3 joins are underlined.

Green plants use sunlight, water, and carbon dioxide to make their own food. This process is called photosynthesis.

1. LOOK
2. PLAN
3. PRACTICE

NOTE:
When joining into **s** use either Join 3 or Join 8.

As a byproduct, they release oxygen which we breathe.

Chara   Dictyota   Pteridium   Zamia

© 2012 Getty-Dubay   27   Getty-Dubay® Italic Handwriting Series · Book E

Getty-Dubay® Cursive Italic Lowercase Joins

JOIN 4: DIAGONAL INTO e

Join 4 is a straight diagonal line to the branching line into the center of **e**.

a → ae
diagonal into e

Trace & copy.
ae | ae ce de ee he ie ke le
ae

VOWEL SOUND:
E: silent

me ne ue ze e hom*e* peopl*e*
me

VOWEL SOUND:
EE: long E
PHONOGRAMS: -ee, -eed

ee eel keep -ee see -eed seed
ee

PHONOGRAMS:

-eek seek -eel heel -eem seem
eek

NOTE:
Join into e at the branching line.

imaginary branching line ···· een

AVOID
ae
↑ scoop

-een seen -eep deep -eer deer

-eet meet -ief chief -ike like
eet

REMINDER: Option: You may join into m, n, and r using Join 2.

OPTIONAL JOIN
-ile mile en seem seen deer
ile

SUFFIX: -ment

-ment environment fragment
ment

✏ Circle one of your best diagonal joins into e.

NOTE: For two-stroke e see INSTRUCTION MANUAL

A source of lead is the mineral galena.

'Lead' in pencils is actually graphite; one of the world's softest minerals.

OPTION: Lift before **e** from baseline.

ae ce de ee he ie ke *or* ke le me ne ue ze
ae

NOTE: When lifting between letters, be sure to keep letters close together.
Joins are natural spacers – when not using a join, keep letters close.

Getty-Dubay® Italic Handwriting Series · Book E   © 2012 Getty-Dubay

Getty-Dubay® Cursive italic Lowercase Joins

REVIEW: JOIN 4

JOIN 4 joins are underlined.

Minerals:
1. naturally occurring
2. inorganic solid
3. crystal structure
4. characteristic chemical composition

M

✏️ Are you joining into **e** at the branching line? Yes___ No___

In the rock cycle, forces within Earth and at the surface cause rocks to change form.

There are three types of rocks: sedimentary, igneous, and metamorphic.

REMINDER:
Relax your hand. Tap your index finger on your pencil three times to help avoid pinching. See Pencil Hold on page vi.

✏️ Circle one of your best diagonal joins into **e**.

When magma reaches the Earth's surface it is called lava, and the lava forms a volcanic mountain.

w

1️⃣ LOOK at your writing.

2️⃣ Pick the joins that need work. Compare them with the models. PLAN how to make the joins look more like the models.

3️⃣ PRACTICE on lined paper.

lava

magma

Getty-Dubay® Cursive italic Lowercase Joins

JOIN 5: HORIZONTAL

*Join 5 is a horizontal join at the waistline. Join out of **o**, **t**, **f**, **v**, **w**, and **x** into every letter except **f**.*

o⃗ o⃗n
horizontal
into soft angle

on | on om or ox com- combine
Trace & copy. on

PREFIXES: com-, con-, mono-

con- connect mono- monorail
con

SUFFIXES: -ion, -or

-ion champion -or author
-ion

VOWEL SOUND:
OR: OR sound
SUFFIX: -dom

or orbit order -dom wisdom
or

ou oy oi oj op ov ow
ou

horizontal
into sharp angle

VOWEL SOUNDS:
OU: OU diphthong
OY: OI diphthong
OI: OI diphthong

ou mountain oy boy oi oil
ou

VOWEL SOUNDS:
OW: long O
OW: OU diphthong

ow grow ow flower
ow

DICOT FLOWER sepals and petals in groups of fours or fives — sedum, dogwood

SUFFIX: -ous

-ous famous
-ous

MONOCOT FLOWER sepals and petals in groups of three or multiples of three — lily

SUFFIX: -ious

NOTE:
Close up the top of **o** so that **o** doesn't look like **u**.

-ious delicious ambitious
-ious

✏️ Circle one of your best joins out of **o**.

PRACTICE here and on lined paper.

Getty-Dubay® Italic Handwriting Series · Book E

Getty-Dubay® Cursive italic Lowercase Joins

ō ōo ōŏ ōa
horizontal
start back

oo oa oc od og oq os
oo

VOWEL SOUNDS:
OO: short OO
OO: long OO

o͝o good book o͞o cool smooth
oo

VOWEL SOUND:
OA: long O
PHONOGRAMS: -oat, -oak, -oan

oa oak boat -oat -oak -oan
oa

ō ōt ōl
horizontal
swing up

ot ol oh ob ok -ology biology
ot

SUFFIX: -ology
PHONOGRAMS:
Write words using these phonograms.

-ob -ock -od -og -oke -old

NOTE: Avoid diagonal into **t**.   ō·t

-one -ong -oo -ood -ook -ool

-oom -oon -oop -oot -op

NOTE: Avoid diagonal into **l, h, b,** and **k**.   ō·l

-ope -ore -orn -ot -ow(ō) -ow(ou)

✏ Are you joining out of **o** with a horizontal line?   Yes____ No____

OPTION: Join into **e** from waistline.

ō ōe
diagonal
into e

oe doe foe hoe roe toe woe Joe Zoe
oe

OPTION: Lift before **e** from waistline.

oe doe foe hoe roe toe woe Joe Zoe
oe

NOTE: When lifting between letters, be sure to keep letters close together.

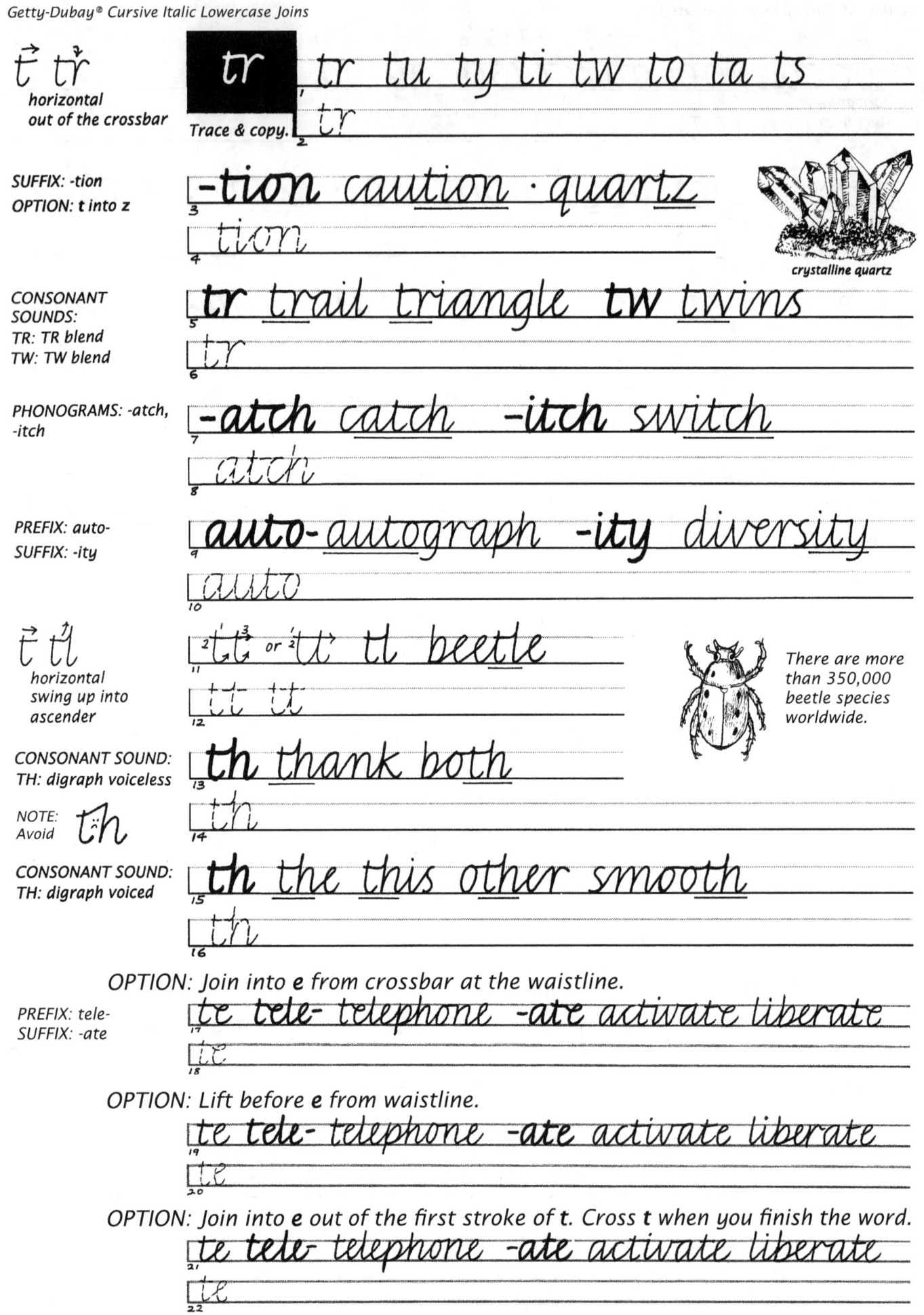

Getty-Dubay® Cursive Italic Lowercase Joins

f **fr**
horizontal
out of the crossbar

fr Trace & copy.

fr fu fy fi fo fa fs
fr

CONSONANT SOUND:
FR: FR blend
SUFFIX: -ify

fr fresh fruit   -ify identify
fr

CONSONANT SOUND:
FL: FL blend

NOTE:
Avoid **fl**

NOTE: Join f and t
with one crossbar.

fl fly   flea   flew
fl

PHONOGRAMS: -aft,
-ift

ft ft ft   -aft craft -ift lift
ft

✏️ Circle one of your best joins out of **f**.

OPTION: Join into **e** from crossbar of **f**.   fe fe   life

OPTION: Lift before **e** after **f**.   fe fe   life

NOTE:
Join into **n**, **m**, **r**, & **x**
used here is the
Diagonal Swing Up
Join.
(See pages 19 and
24.)

"Every part of this earth is sacred to my
people. Every shining pine needle, every
sandy shore, every mist in the dark
woods, every clearing, and every
humming insect is holy in the memory
of my people.... All things are connected."
                                  —Chief Seattle

Excerpts from a letter
to President Pierce
written in 1855 and
attributed to Chief
Seattle, Duwamish
tribe, state of
Washington.

Getty-Dubay® Cursive Italic Lowercase Joins

v⃗ vn horizontal

vn | vn vu vy vi vo va vs vt
Trace & copy. vn

v⃘ ve diagonal into e
PHONOGRAMS: -ave, -ive, -ove
SUFFIXES: -ive, -ves

ve -ave save -ive live -ove love
ve
-ive active -ves calves hooves
ive

w⃗ wn horizontal

wn | wn wr wu wy wo wa ws
wn

CONSONANT SOUND:
WR: R sound
PHONOGRAMS: -awn, -own

wr write -awn dawn -own town
wr

PHONOGRAM: -owl
NOTE: Avoid wl

wt wl wh wk -owl howl
wt

CONSONANT SOUND:
WH: digraph (HW blend)
PHONOGRAM: -awk

wh whale -awk hawk
wh

w⃘ we diagonal into e

we web well wet
we

Zone-tailed hawk

✏ Circle one of your best joins out of **v** and out of **w**.

x⃗ xu horizontal

xu | xu xy xi xo xa xt xl xe

x⃘ xe diagonal into e

✏ Circle one of your best joins out of **x**.

OPTION: Lift before **e** from waistline.

ve ve   we we   xe xe

Getty-Dubay® Italic Handwriting Series · Book E

Getty-Dubay® Cursive Italic Lowercase Joins

REVIEW: JOIN 5

JOIN 5 joins are underlined.

> The Earth is divided into seven continents: Africa, Antarctica, Asia, Australia, Europe, North America, and South America.

NOTE:
In this paragraph, the join from the baseline into **n**, **m**, **r**, and **x** is Join 2, shown on pages 19 and 24.

> Biome: a large region characterized by a specific kind of climate and certain kinds of plant and animal communities.

Aquatic biome is split into freshwater and marine.

> The terrestrial biomes (land) are: alpine, desert, tundra, rainforest, temperate forest, chaparral, taiga, savanna, and temperate grasslands.

1. LOOK at your writing CHECKLIST
___ letter shape
___ letter size
___ letter slope
___ letter spacing

2. PLAN how to make the joins look more like the models.

3. PRACTICE on lined paper.

Getty-Dubay® Italic Handwriting Series · Book E

Getty-Dubay® Cursive Italic Lowercase Joins

JOIN 6: DIAGONAL OUT OF r

Join 6 is a short diagonal line out of r into all letters except f.

r r̃n
diagonal

Trace & copy. rn rn rm rr ru ry ri rp ro
rn

PHONOGRAMS: -arm, -orn, -urn

ra rc rd rs -arm alarm
ra

NOTE: Bend arm of r at the waistline before joining.
AVOID rn looking like m

-orn horn -urn Saturn
orn

Saturn's rings of whirling ice.

SUFFIXES: -ary, -arium

-ary library -arium aquarium
ary

PHONOGRAMS: -ard, -arp, -arn

-ard card -arp harp -arn barn
ard

PHONOGRAMS: -art, -irt, -ort, -url, -ark, -ork.

rt rl rh rb rk re -art smart
rt

-irt shirt -ort sport -url curl
irt

Double r

-ark mark -ork fork rr error
ark

PREFIX: re-
PHONOGRAMS: -are, -ore

re rewrite -are care -ore more
re

✏ Circle one of your best joins out of r.

OPTION: Lift after r.

NOTE: When lifting after r, keep letters close together.

rn rm rr ru ry ri rp ro re ra rc rd rg rs rt

Getty-Dubay® Italic Handwriting Series · Book E   36   © 2012 Getty-Dubay

Getty-Dubay® Cursive Italic Lowercase Joins

SUFFIXES: -ward, -ern, -ry, -ery

-ward forward -ern western
ward

NOTE:
The join out of **r** needs more practice than any other join. Legibility depends on it being done well.

-ry poetry -ery pottery
ry

REVIEW: JOIN 6

JOIN 6 joins are underlined.

    There are eight planets in our solar system. In order of their closeness to the sun, they are: Mercury, Venus, Earth, Mars, Jupiter, Saturn, Uranus, and Neptune.

Pluto is now considered a dwarf planet or planetoid according to the International Astronomical Union, August, 2006. Due to its orbital path, Pluto is sometimes closer to the sun than Neptune.

Pluto is now a dwarf planet/planetoid.

Our planet Earth is about 150 million kilometers from the sun. This distance is equal to one astronomical unit.

1. **LOOK** at your writing.
2. **PLAN** which letters need work. Compare them with the models.
3. **PRACTICE** on lined paper.

REMINDER: Tap your index finger on the pencil three times to help avoid pinching. See Pencil Hold on page vi.

Pluto*
Neptune
Uranus
Saturn
Jupiter
Mars
Earth
Venus
Mercury
sun

© 2012 Getty-Dubay   Getty-Dubay® Italic Handwriting Series · Book E

Getty-Dubay® Cursive Italic Lowercase Joins

JOIN 7: HORIZONTAL TO DIAGONAL

Join 7 is a horizontal line at the baseline blending into a diagonal line. Follow back out of **s**, **b**, and **p** and join into all letters except **f** and **z**.

s *sn*
→
horizontal
to diagonal

Trace & copy.

sn | sn sm su sy si sp sw so
sn

se st sl sh sk or sk ss or ss
se

CONSONANT SOUNDS:
SN: SN blend
SM: SM blend

sn snow snail sm smile smart
sn

SP: SP blend
SW: SW blend

sp space respond sw swim swirl
sp

ST: ST blend
SL: SL blend

st story best sl slope slant
st

SH: digraph
SK: SK blend

sh shape finish sk sky task
sh

SUFFIXES: -less, -est, -ist, -ship, -ism, -ness

-less homeless -est smallest
-less

-ist artist -ship friendship
-ist

-ism heroism -ness happiness
-ism

✎ Circle one of your best joins out of s.

PRACTICE here and on lined paper.

Getty-Dubay® Italic Handwriting Series · Book E

Getty-Dubay® Cursive Italic Lowercase Joins

b b∧n
horizontal to diagonal

br Trace & copy.
br bu by bi bl bb bo be

CONSONANT SOUNDS:
BR: BR blend
BL: BL blend
Double **b**

br library bl blend bb bubble

p p∧n
horizontal to diagonal

pr
pr pu py pi pl pp po pe

CONSONANT SOUNDS:
PR: PR blend
PL: PL blend
PH: F sound
PREFIX: pro-
Double **p**

pr practice improve pl please

ph photo pro-protect pp apple

✎ Circle one of your best joins out of **b** and out of **p**.

REVIEW: JOIN 7

JOIN 7 joins are underlined.

Our solar system consists of one star which we call the sun, eight planets and their moons, an asteroid belt (10,000 and counting), and other objects moving through the solar system such as comets and meteoroids.

OPTION: Lift after **s**, **b**, and **p**. ss bb pp sn br pr

NOTE: When lifting after **s**, **b** and **p** keep letters close.

sa se si so su · ba be bi bo bu · pa pe pi po pu

© 2012 Getty-Dubay   Getty-Dubay® Italic Handwriting Series · Book E

Getty-Dubay® Cursive Italic Lowercase Joins

JOIN 8: DIAGONAL TO HORIZONTAL

Join 8 is a diagonal line from the baseline blending into a horizontal line at the waistline. Join into a, c, d, g, q, and s.

a/ aa
diagonal to horizontal

aa aa ca da ea ha ia ka la
Trace & copy. aa

NOTE:
Close up the top of **a** so that **a** doesn't look like **u**.

ma na ua za sa ba pa
ma

VOWEL SOUNDS:
EA: long E
EA: short E sound

ea east neat sea ea weather
ea

PHONOGRAMS: Write a word using each phonogram.

-eak -eal -eam -ear -eat

Silent c

-ace -ack -ice   c science

SUFFIX: -ian

-ian musician mathematician
ian

✏ Circle one of your best joins into **a**.

a/ ac
diagonal to horizontal

Double c
ac ac ec ic uc sc cc accept
ac

CONSONANT SOUND:
SC: SC blend

sc school telescope describe
sc

✏ Circle one of your best joins into **c**.

PRACTICE here and on lined paper.

Getty-Dubay® Cursive Italic Lowercase Joins

a/ ad
diagonal to horizontal

Double d

ad | ad ed id ud **dd** addition

Trace & copy. ad

PHONOGRAMS: Write a word using each phonogram.

-ad -ade -ed -eed -id -ide

SUFFIX:

-and -end -ind -ed challenged

NOTE: Close up the top of **d** so that **d** doesn't look like **cl**.

d d

✏ Circle one of your best joins into **d**.

a/ ag aq
diagonal to horizontal

ag aq | ag eg ig ug aq eq iq

ag

CONSONANT SOUND:
NG: NG

ng sing length -ang -ing

ng

PHONOGRAMS: Write a word using each phonogram.

-ung -ag -ig -ug -eg

CONSONANT SOUND:
Q: KW sound

qu quiet equal qu

✏ Circle your best join into **g** and into **q**.

NOTE: Close up the top of **g** and **q** so that they don't look like **y**.

g g
q q

Most comets travel in a highly elliptical orbit around the sun.

This is part of the 200 ft. long Bayeux tapestry.

Halley's comet appeared in 1066 as recorded in the Bayeux tapestry embroidered in the 11th century. This comet has been recorded since 240 B.C. and appears every 75 to 76 years. It last appeared in 1986 and will return in 2061.

© 2012 Getty-Dubay — 41 — Getty-Dubay® Italic Handwriting Series · Book E

Getty-Dubay® Cursive Italic Lowercase Joins

a/ as
diagonal to horizontal

as Double s
as es is us ss success

Trace & copy.
as

PHONOGRAMS: Write a word using each phonogram.

-ase -ash -ask -ast -est -ise

NOTE:
AVOID wave
is

-ish -isk -us -ush -ust

REVIEW: JOIN 8

JOIN 8 joins are underlined.

Galaxy: a large group of individual systems, star clusters, dust and gas bound together by gravity.

OPTION: Lift before **a, c, d, g, q,** and **s** when joining from the baseline.

aa ea ia ua · ac ec ic uc · ad ed id ud
aa

ag eg ig ug · aq eq iq uq · as es is us
ag

NOTE:
All optional joins & lifts are used here:
Join 2 into **n, m, r** and **x**;
lift before **e**,
lift after **r**,
lift after **s, b, & p**;
lift before **a, c, d, g, q,** and **s**.

Galaxy: a large group of individual systems, star clusters, dust and gas bound together by gravity.

Shapes of galaxies: Ellipticals, Spirals (Milky Way), Barred spirals, and Irregulars.
(left to right)

Getty-Dubay® Cursive Italic Lowercase Joins

LIFTS: Lift before f and lift before z from baseline; lift after g, j, q, and y.

NOTE:
Joins are natural spacers. When letters are not joined, place letters close together. AVOID gap.

af az   af az ef ez if iz of oz
af

Double f
Double z

ff off zz pizza ff

ga ju qu yu   ga ju qu yu
ga

CONSONANT SOUNDS:
GH: silent
GL: GL blend

gh light neighbor gl globe glass
gr

GR: GR blend
Double g

gr agree gravity gg juggle eggs
gr

CONSONANT SOUNDS:
G: regular
G: J sound
J: regular
Q: KW sound
Y: consonant
Y: long E
Y: long I

g go g gym j join q quiet y you
g

y everyone y myself e

✏️ When lifting are you keeping letters close together to AVOID gaps?   Yes___ No___

NOTE: When lifting between letters, be sure to keep letters close together.
Joins are natural spacers -- when not using a join, keep letters close.

NOTE:
All optional joins & lifts are used here:
Join 2 into **n, m, r** and **x**;
lift before **e**,
lift after **r**,
lift after **s, b,** & **p**;
lift before **a, c, d, g, q,** and **s**.

Beyond our galaxy in all directions
exist countless other galaxies. The
Hubble Telescope is providing us with
views describing the vastness of the
Universe.

waistline → B

BASELINE ONLY: Write on the baseline and imagine where the waistline is. (It is halfway between the baselines.)

© 2012 Getty-Dubay   43   Getty-Dubay® Italic Handwriting Series · Book E

Getty-Dubay® Cursive Italic

SIZE: 4mm bodyheight; 6mm capital and ascender height and descender length

body height 4mm *A quick brown fox jumps over the lazy dog.*

A

OPTIONAL JOIN

br um er

✏️ Are your letters the correct height?   Yes____   No____

5° SLOPE:
Write your signature using cursive italic. Write names of your family: mother, father, sisters, brothers, grandparents, aunts or uncles.

✏️ Are your downstrokes parallel to the slope lines?   Yes____   No____

SPACING: Use even spacing in words. Joins are natural spacers. When letters are not joined, place letters close together.

Write your signature using cursive italic.

✏️ Are you spacing the letters evenly?   Yes____   No____

CHECKLIST
____ letter shape
____ letter size
____ letter slope
____ letter spacing

BASELINE ONLY: Write on the baseline and imagine where the waistline is. (It is halfway between the baselines.)

AVOID tangling capitals, ascenders, and descenders.

✏️ Is your handwriting getting better?   Yes____   No____

Getty-Dubay® Italic Handwriting Series · Book E   © 2012 Getty-Dubay

Getty-Dubay® Slope and Speed Guidelines

SLOPE GUIDELINES:

A 5° letter slope is used for basic and cursive.

OPTIONS: You have a choice of slope--from a vertical of 0° to a slope of 15°.
This is the choice range:

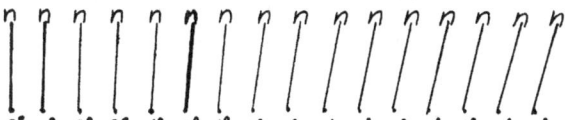

Which is your most comfortable letter slope? Whichever letter slope you choose, use that slope for all your writing.

LOOK at your writing.

✎ Do you have an even letter slope?   Yes___ No___

SLOPE GUIDE:

Make your own slope guide to fit your choice of letter slope. Place a sheet of notebook paper at an angle under your writing paper and line up the lines with your letter slope.

✎ Do your letters have different slopes?   Yes___ No___

PLAN how to write with an even letter slope. Use the following exercise to find a comfortable slope for you.

1. write word — *slope*
2. draw slope lines over letters — *slope*
3. pick one slope — *slope*
4. draw parallel lines — ////////
5. write over slope lines — *slope*

Choose a letter slope and write all your letters using that slope.

Use paper clips or removable tape to hold the two sheets together. On the undersheet outline the edge of the writing paper so you know where to place the next sheet of paper.

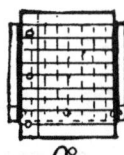 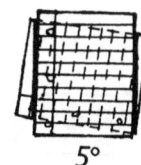 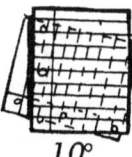 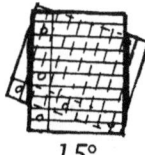
 0°   5°   10°   15°

SPEED: TIMED WRITING   Use the timed writing to help increase speed.
The goal is to increase the number of words written per minute.
Begin by writing the following sentence (or another sentence) as a warm-up.

A quick brown fox jumps over the lazy dog.

1. TIME LENGTH: 1 MINUTE Write the sentence at your most comfortable speed. If you finish before the time is up, begin the sentence again. Count the number of words written. Write this number in the margin.
2. TIME LENGTH: 1 MINUTE Write the sentence a little faster. Try to add one or two more words to your total. Count the number of words written.
3. TIME LENGTH: 1 MINUTE Write the sentence as fast as you can. Count the number of words written.
4. TIME LENGTH: 1 MINUTE Write the sentence at a comfortable speed. Count the number of words written. Write the number in the margin.

Repeat process once a month.   ✎ Compare the total of # 4 to # 1.
Did you increase the number of words written by one or more? Yes___ No___

EYES CLOSED   Using the same sentence, do this exercise as a follow-up to the timed writing. Use a non-lined sheet of paper. Close your eyes. Picture in your mind's eye the shape of each letter as you write. Take all the time you need.
You may be amazed how well you can write with your eyes closed.

© 2012 Getty-Dubay

GETTY-DUBAY® BASIC ITALIC CAPITALS & CURSIVE ITALIC CAPITALS

	EGYPTIAN HIEROGLYPH	PHOENICIAN LETTER	GREEK LETTER	ROMAN LETTER	BASIC ITALIC	CURSIVE ITALIC CAPITAL

A — 5° slope
1st stroke: curve exit serif
3rd stroke: extended entrance of crossbar

OX

Ghana — *Accra* India — *Agra* Turkey — *Ankara* Georgia — *Atlanta*

other cities beginning with A

B — 2nd stroke: curve entrance serif

HOUSE

Thailand — *Bangkok* Lebanon — *Beirut* Germany — *Berlin* Massachusetts — *Boston*

other cities beginning with B

C — no change

CAMEL

India — *Calcutta* Colombia — *Cali* Venezuela — *Caracas* Illinois — *Chicago*

other cities beginning with C

D — 2nd stroke: curve entrance serif

DOOR

India — *Delhi* Colorado — *Denver* Indonesia — *Djakarta* Ireland — *Dublin*

other cities beginning with D

1. LOOK
2. PLAN
3. PRACTICE

✏️ Circle some of your best capitals.

CHECKLIST
___ letter shape
___ letter size
___ letter slope
___ letter spacing

Getty-Dubay® Italic Handwriting Series · Book E

Getty-Dubay® Basic Italic & Cursive Italic Capitals

	EGYPTIAN HIEROGLYPH	PHOENICIAN LETTER	GREEK LETTER	ROMAN LETTER	BASIC ITALIC	CURSIVE ITALIC CAPITAL

E — 2nd stroke: curve entrance serif

Hieroglyph: 𓀠 — Phoenician: ⴲ (BEHOLD) — Greek: Ǝ — Roman: E — Basic Italic: E — Cursive: E ↓ — ₃→ or E

Scotland — Canada — Texas — Germany
Edinburgh Edmonton El Paso Essen

other cities beginning with E

F — 2nd stroke: curve entrance serif

Phoenician: Y (HOOK/NAIL) — Greek: F — Roman: F — Basic Italic: F — Cursive: F ↓ — ₃→ or F

Italy — Brazil — Germany — China
Florence Fortaleza Frankfurt Fushon

other cities beginning with F

G — changes to one-stroke: curve exit serif

(Added in the 3rd century B.C. The Romans added a bar to C to form G.) — Basic Italic: G — Cursive: G or G

Italy — Belgium — Scotland — Switzerland
Genoa Ghent Glasgow Geneva

other cities beginning with G

H
- 1st stroke: sharp angle entrance serif, curve exit serif
- 2nd stroke: curve entrance serif begins slightly higher
- 3rd stroke: extended crossbar

Phoenician: H (FENCE) — Greek: H — Roman: H — Basic Italic: H — Cursive: H

China — Finland — Hawaii — China
Hangchou Helsinki Honolulu Hsian

other cities beginning with H

1. LOOK
2. PLAN
3. PRACTICE

CHECKLIST
___ letter shape
___ letter size
___ letter slope
___ letter spacing

✏ Circle some of your best capitals.

© 2012 Getty-Dubay   47   Getty-Dubay® Italic Handwriting Series · Book E

Getty-Dubay® Basic Italic & Cursive Italic Capitals

	EGYPTIAN HIEROGLYPH	PHOENICIAN LETTER	GREEK LETTER	ROMAN LETTER	BASIC ITALIC	CURSIVE ITALIC CAPITAL

I — changes to one-stroke: horizontal entrance serif and exit serif

⟨hand⟩   ⟨z⟩   ⟨ʃ⟩   I   I   I I or J

South Korea   *India*   *Turkey*   *Indiana*

Inchon Indore Istanbul Indianapolis

other cities beginning with I

J — one stroke: horizontal entrance serif

(Added in the 16th century.)   J or J   J J or J

Florida   *India*   *Saudi Arabia*

Jacksonville Jaipur Jerusalem Juddah

other cities beginning with J

K — 1st stroke: sharp angle entrance serif, curve exit serif; 2nd stroke: curve exit serif

⟨palm⟩   ⟨Y⟩   K   K   K K K K

Pakistan   *Russia*   *Jamaica*   *Japan*

Karachi Kharkov Kingston Kyoto

other cities beginning with K

L — one stroke: curve entrance serif, short exit serif

⟨ox goad⟩   L   Γ·L   L   L L or L

Nigeria   *Peru*   *Portugal*   *England*

Lagos Lima Lisbon Liverpool

other cities beginning with L

1. LOOK
2. PLAN
3. PRACTICE

✏ Circle some of your best capitals.

CHECKLIST
___ letter shape
___ letter size
___ letter slope
___ letter spacing

Getty-Dubay® Basic Italic & Cursive Italic Capitals

| EGYPTIAN HIEROGLYPH | PHOENICIAN LETTER | GREEK LETTER | ROMAN LETTER | BASIC ITALIC | CURSIVE ITALIC CAPITAL |

M — 1st stroke: curve exit serif

WATER

Spain — *Madrid* Philippines — *Manila* Tennessee — *Memphis* Russia — *Moscow*

other cities beginning with M

N — 1st stroke: curve exit serif; 3rd stroke: soft curve entrance serif begins slightly higher

FISH

NOTE: 3rd stroke begins higher

India — *Nagpur* Kenya — *Nairobi* China — *Nanking* New Jersey — *Newark*

other cities beginning with N

O — no changes

EYE

Nebraska — *Omaha* Japan — *Osaka* Norway — *Oslo* Canada — *Ottawa*

other cities beginning with O

P — 2nd stroke: curve entrance serif

MOUTH

France — *Paris* California — *Pasadena* Oregon — *Portland* Czech Republic — *Prague*

other cities beginning with P

1. LOOK
2. PLAN
3. PRACTICE

CHECKLIST
___ letter shape
___ letter size
___ letter slope
___ letter spacing

✏ Circle some of your best capitals.

© 2012 Getty-Dubay

Getty-Dubay® Basic Italic & Cursive Italic Capitals

| EGYPTIAN HIEROGLYPH | PHOENICIAN LETTER | GREEK LETTER | ROMAN LETTER | BASIC ITALIC | CURSIVE ITALIC CAPITAL |

Q — 2nd stroke: short exit serif

KNOT

Canada — Quebec Philippines — Quezon City Ecuador — Quito Massachusetts — Quincy

other cities beginning with Q

R — 2nd stroke: curve entrance serif; 3rd stroke: soft curve exit serif

HEAD

Morocco — Rabat Brazil — Recife New York — Rochester Italy — Rome

other cities beginning with R

S — no changes

TOOTH

Japan — Sapporo Washington — Seattle Egypt — Suez Australia — Sydney

other cities beginning with S

T — 2nd stroke: curve entrance serif

MARK/SIGN

Japan — Tokyo Ohio — Toledo Canada — Toronto Italy — Turin

other cities beginning with T

1. LOOK
2. PLAN
3. PRACTICE

✏️ Circle some of your best capitals.

CHECKLIST
___ letter shape
___ letter size
___ letter slope
___ letter spacing

Getty-Dubay® Italic Handwriting Series · Book E   50   © 2012 Getty-Dubay

Getty-Dubay® Basic Italic & Cursive Italic Capitals

| | EGYPTIAN HIEROGLYPH | PHOENICIAN LETTER | GREEK LETTER | ROMAN LETTER | BASIC ITALIC | CURSIVE ITALIC CAPITAL |

one-stroke: soft angle entrance serif

(Added in the 16th century.) U U U

Ufa (Russia) Ulan Bator (Mongolia) Utica (New York) Utrecht (The Netherlands)

other cities beginning with U

one-stroke: curve entrance serif

Y F V V V V   HOOK/NAIL

Valparaiso (Chile) Vancouver (Canada) Venice (Italy) Vienna (Austria)

other cities beginning with V

one-stroke: curve entrance serif

(Added in the 11th century.) W W W

Warsaw (Poland) Washington (District of Columbia) Winnipeg (Canada)

other cities beginning with W

1st stroke: curve entrance serif and exit serif

⚌ X X X X X
PROP

Xanthi (Greece) Xenia (Ohio) Xilitla (Mexico) Xochimilco (Mexico)

other cities beginning with X

1. LOOK
2. PLAN
3. PRACTICE

✏️ Circle some of your best capitals.

CHECKLIST
___ letter shape
___ letter size
___ letter slope
___ letter spacing

© 2012 Getty-Dubay

Getty-Dubay® Basic Italic & Cursive Italic Capitals

| LOOK | PLAN | PRACTICE |

CHECKLIST
___ shape
___ size
___ slope
___ spacing

✏️ Circle some of your best capitals.

✏️ How is your handwriting getting better?

TIMELINE

Egyptian — Phoenician — Early Greek — Classical Greek — Roman — Italic
3000 2500 2000 1500 1000 500 B.C. 0 500 A.D. 1000 1500 2000

NOTE: For basic & cursive capital assessment questions see INSTRUCTION MANUAL.

CONGRATULATIONS! You have completed this book. You are improving your handwriting day by day. Good Work!

As you write on your own, continue to practice good handwriting habits: even slope, even size, and even spacing. Hooray for you and your good handwriting!

✏️ Turn to page viii and write your Post-test. Use your best cursive italic handwriting.

SPECIAL ASSIGNMENT: WRITE A LETTER/BOOKLET

Write a letter to a relative, a friend, or a pen-pal.

ROUGH DRAFT: *Compose your letter in pencil. Use lined paper or 4mm lines on page 56.*

CHECK WORDING: *Edit for capitals, spelling and punctuation.*

BOOKLET: *Make the surprise booklet.*

Materials: sheet of light or medium weight paper and scissors. A 28 cm x 43 cm (11" x 17") sheet will give a finished size of 10.8 cm x 14 cm (4 1/4" x 5 1/2"). This size will fit an A-2 envelope.

NOTE: In illustrations dotted line indicates fold that occurs within the given step. Solid lines within rectangle indicate folds previously established.

1. Fold AB to CD to establish EF.
2. Open back to original size.
3. Fold AC to BD to establish GH.
4. Fold GH to AC/BD to establish IJ.
5. Open to previous fold (GH/AB/CD).
6. With scissors, cut KL by cutting halfway between GH, stopping at fold IJ.
7. Open to original size ABCD.
8. Refold AB to CD as in #1.
9. Grasp E/AC with left hand and F/BD with right hand, then push hands together, establishing 3 pages on one side and 1 on the other.
10. Fold remaining leaf over the other three pages. Two leaves have folds at the top and two on the fore edge of the booklet.

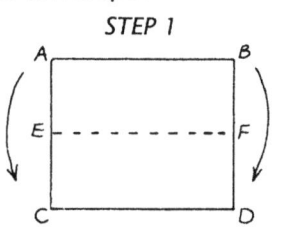
STEP 1

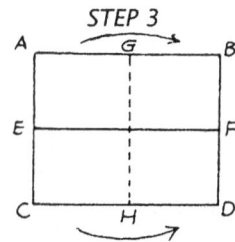
STEP 3

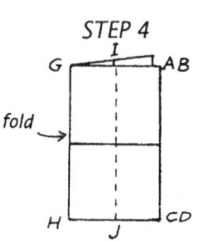
STEP 4

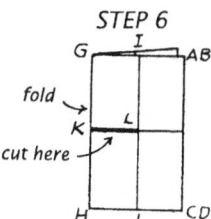
STEP 6

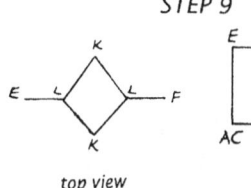
STEP 9 — top view

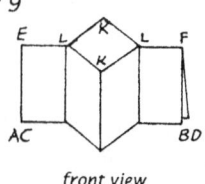
front view

STEP 10

completed booklet

beginning of letter

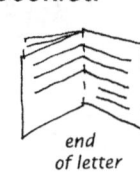
middle of letter

end of letter

Arrange letters on the three two-page spreads of the letter/card. Leave a one inch margin on all sides. Decorate the cover with a design, perhaps using the name of the person the letter is for.

FINAL COPY: *Use your best handwriting for your final copy. Take your time. Write your final copy with a pencil or pen.*

ENVELOPE: *Address the envelope using your best handwriting. On the **first line**, write the name of the person to whom you are writing. On the **second line**, write the person's house number and street name (or Post Office Box number). Add an apartment number, office number, etc. as needed. On the **third line**, write the city, state or province, and postal code. Add country if mailing overseas.*

NOTE: For an envelope template see INSTRUCTION MANUAL.

Take an envelope apart. Spread it out and place on a larger piece of paper.

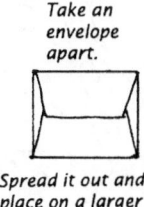

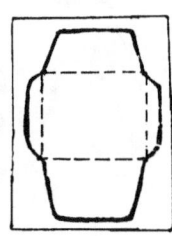

Trace around the edge. Cut out the new envelope. Fold envelope. Glue or tape to hold together.

glue or tape

In the upper left hand corner write your return address.

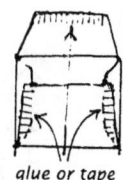

READING LOOPED CURSIVE
COMPARING GETTY-DUBAY® CURSIVE ITALIC WITH LOOPED CURSIVE

Comparing Cursive Italic with Looped Cursive
NOTE: letter shape, letter slope, and size of capitals, ascenders, and descenders

Look at the examples of cursive italic and looped cursive. Compare the two styles of writing. Notice the differences in letter shape, letter slope, capital height, ascender height, and descender length.

There are many styles of writing you need to be able to read. Practice reading looped cursive. To help read the looped cursive letters, each name contains both a capital letter and its lowercase version.

SHAPE:
Look at the different shapes of the looped cursive lowercase letters **b, f, r, s,** and **z** and the capital letters **F, G, I, J, Q, S, T, V, X,** and **Z**.

SLOPE:
Look at the slope difference. Cursive Italic letter slope is 5° and looped cursive is 30°.

SIZE:
Look at the size difference. Cursive italic capitals, ascenders, and descenders are 1 1/2 body heights. Looped cursive capitals, ascenders and descenders are 2 body heights.

Compare the absence of loops in cursive italic with the many loops in looped cursive. Look at how the capitals, ascenders, and descenders become tangled in the looped cursive.
Loop-free italic is easier to read.

CURSIVE ITALIC (5° slope)	LOOPED CURSIVE (30° slope)
Angela	Angela
Barbara	Barbara
Cecilia	Cecilia
David	David
Eugene	Eugene
Fifi	Fifi
Gregory	Gregory
Hannah	Hannah
Irving	Irving
Jojo	Jojo
Kirk	Kirk
Lillian	Lillian
Malcolm	Malcolm
Nancy	Nancy
Otto	Otto
Philippa	Philippa
Queequeg	Queequeg
Richard	Richard
Susan	Susan
Trent	Trent
Ursula	Ursula
Vivian	Vivian
Woodrow	Woodrow
Xerxes	Xerxes
Yonny	Yonny
Zanzi	Zanzi

5mm lines

4mm lines

www.ingramcontent.com/pod-product-compliance
Lightning Source LLC
Chambersburg PA
CBHW060518300426
44112CB00017B/2730